THE YOUNG SPORTSMAN'S GUIDE TO GOLF

THE

YOUNG SPORTSMAN'S GUIDE

TO

GOLF

by

Don Smith

THOMAS NELSON & SONS

Edinburgh   NEW YORK   *Toronto*

ACKNOWLEDGMENTS

The author wishes to express his sincere appreciation to Don Rodda for his help in the editing and preparation of this manuscript.

Thanks also are due to Miss Patti Gallagher of Fort Hamilton High School, a dedicated young lady of the links; Tommy Whitfield, a very fine teen-age player who represents Flushing High School, and Steve Cribari, a star of the future, who posed for the pictures on the following pages.

Also to Buck Worsham, head professional at the Pelham Country Club, and his assistant, Bud Whiting, for making this beautiful golf course available for picture-taking.

And last but not least to Daniel R. Rubin for his wonderful photography.

Contents

Chapter I

Golf Can Be Fun

There never has been a golfer like Bobby Jones.

Even today, 30 years after the Little Emperor stepped out of the spotlight, his legendary feats are familiar to all who play the game.

In an era which produced such great champions as Jack Dempsey and Babe Ruth, Red Grange and Jim Thorpe, the boyish Jones was perhaps an even greater sporting idol. The magic he worked with his flawless golf swing was admired by millions the world over.

Bobby won his first championship in 1911 at the age of eleven. He was still winning titles when he retired at the still-youthful age of 28. He finished first in 13 of 27 national tournaments and defeated the greatest golfers of his time. Jones held every major title golf had to offer. He was the master.

Thus, when Jones decided to retire from golf, fans in all parts of the world refused to believe he was through.

Why? How could the great champion quit? And at such a time...

Bobby had just accomplished his amazing Grand Slam. He won the British Amateur and British Open championships. Then he came home and took the United States Amateur and Open championships. No one in the history of the ancient game ever had been good enough to achieve this pinnacle. Yet Jones announced he was quitting at the very peak of his brilliant career.

Why? The answer was simple—to Jones.

"Golf is no longer fun," he said. "I started playing in tournaments because I enjoyed them. I continued playing for the same reason. But now, well, it is no longer fun. So, it's time to quit."

None of us likely ever will be a Bobby Jones. Golfers of his brilliance flash across the horizon just once in a lifetime. But he has left a message that all of us would-be golfers should keep in mind:

Golf should be fun!

Any boy taking up golf will find much is to be gained by heeding the great Jones' advice. His words are as true today as they were then. Play for fun. Think of golf as a game—a healthy, wholesome game. You will enjoy it for years to come.

Golf is an everyday job with the professionals—just as going to school is your job or going to the office is your dad's job. The pros must win to earn money. They make their living that way. And yet, most of them have not lost sight of the fact that golf is a game.

Doug Ford, one of the leading money-winners in golf, sums it up best when he says, "The pro who takes golf too seriously cannot last long. It is a game, a sport, a pleasure."

Let the pros play for money. We will play for enjoyment and relaxation. If we can't be champions like Bobby Jones, at least we can have a good time playing the game. You don't have to be a winner to enjoy golf.

An instructor can teach you the fundamentals of swinging a club but he can't teach you to enjoy the game. That part is up to you. So, take a great champion's advice and *have fun on the golf course*.

Once you have learned that having fun is the main purpose of golf, you are ready to start exploring the other pleasures the game holds in store for you.

As a new golfer, you might well consider that this is a lifetime proposition. Golf knows no age limits.

In many other sports, athletes are "over the hill" at a time when most golfers are just learning what the game is all about. Professional boxers, football players and tennis stars, for example, are considered "old" when they reach 30. Baseball players are about the same.

Swimming is even more demanding. Many Olympic swimming champions retire before their twentieth birthdays! Beyond that, the arduous and punishing schedule needed to stay in championship condition is more than their bodies can stand. Ice skaters don't last much longer.

But golfers, fortunately, can go on as long as they feel like playing. Age and physical condition are not all-important. You don't have to be young to master golf—or to enjoy it. It is not a sport of brute force or speed. It does not provide great advantages for one person on the basis of size or strength.

By its very nature, golf is a great equalizer. So many skills and attributes can be brought to bear that it automatically balances the scales between young and old, strong and not so strong, the vigorous and the leisurely. A young man might hit the ball farther than his older partner. But the senior man's experience might cancel out the booming drives...So it goes, with the beginner or the professional.

Great ones like Sam Snead, Ben Hogan, Jimmy Demaret and Lloyd Mangrum are all 50 years old—or close to it. And yet they continually take the measure of younger and stronger men on the pro tour. Age has dimmed neither their skill nor their zest for the game.

Size counts little among the pros. Many of the top stars are small fellows—Paul Harney, Bob Toski, Gene Littler and Jerry Barber, to mention a few. None of them weighs more than 160 pounds and yet they are seldom far behind six-foot-six 250-pound George Bayer when it comes to driving a ball off the tee.

It is easy to see, then, that you can enjoy golf even though you may lack the size to play football, basketball or baseball—or any other game in which height and weight are important factors.

Although physical attributes do not play a major part in golf, it nevertheless is a body-building game. Growing youngsters can hasten the development of their bodies by frequent trips to the course.

Of course, this development might not be as easily seen as the bulging muscles of a weight-lifter. But swinging a golf club is a fine way to strengthen your hands, wrists, arms and shoulders since so many parts of your body are brought into play. Walking up and down hills during a round of golf helps to condition other parts of your body, particularly your legs. And, as dad might tell you, the healthful exercise is a grand way to keep the waistline trim.

Because golf is not essentially a contact game, it has become very popular with girls, whose usual sports are basketball, volleyball and swimming. Much to their delight, the ladies are discovering that in many cases they can compete on even terms with male golfers of a comparable age. Indeed, it is not at all uncommon to hear of the girls getting the better of it in junior matches.

The popularity of golf with the girls is clearly indicated on the membership rolls of clubs throughout the country. A few years ago, relatively few of them took part in the sport. Today, there are hundreds of junior tournaments exclusively for the girls. And more young ladies are found on the public courses, too.

This increased popularity of girls' golf can be traced to the growth of women's professional golf.

Major tournaments involving talented women stars like Mickey Wright, Patty Berg, Louise Suggs and Betsy Rawls have done much to attract others to the sport. Television and newspapers keep bringing women's golf right into the home, further stimulating interest.

And speaking of the home, golf is a sport which provides the whole family with a chance to play together. It is not at all unusual to see mother and dad and the children enjoying themselves as a group at the local course.

Also, father-son and husband-wife tournaments have proved extremely popular in the yearly programs of many private clubs.

In view of the great numbers of boys and girls who are playing golf, the game offers the beginner some fine opportunities to make new friends and acquaintances. It is easy to make friends on the golf course because other beginners are sharing the same experiences with you. Thus, you have plenty to talk about. And, if you've learned to enjoy golf, there's always plenty to laugh about.

You will find this holds true in later years as well. Golf is a fine social meeting ground. It opens many doors because those who play are bound together by a common—and fascinating—interest.

Boys can make money in golf too—by working after school and on weekends as caddies.

Caddying provides a golfing education all its own. More important than the money to be made is the wealth of knowledge and golfing experience a boy gets by serving as a bag-carrier.

Many of the top pro golfers, including Ben Hogan, perhaps the greatest since Bobby Jones, got their starts this way.

"Next to playing," says Hogan, "caddying is the best way for a youngster to get acquainted with golf."

As Hogan says, caddying enables you to become an intimate part of the game. You see all types of golf swings, good and bad. You have a chance to observe from close range the way good players make winning shots. You can copy individual styles and perhaps choose one that suits yourself.

What other sport affords you the opportunity to walk around with its best players, and study their movements and strategy? What other game puts you right in the middle of the competition even though you are not a competitor?

Doug Ford, a champion, started as a caddy years ago. To this day, he believes it was the greatest thing that ever happened to him. Ford says, "After a month or so of caddying, I had the equivalent of a year of instruction."

The experience you gain by caddying may pay rich dividends in later years. Colleges and universities are always on the look-out for youngsters with golfing backgrounds. The lad who learns golfing fundamentals by caddying stands a good chance of earning a scholarship to one of the big universities.

Any numbers of today's ranking professional players might never have been able to attend college had it not been for their early schooling as caddies—which developed their ability to hit a golf ball straighter and farther than other boys.

Colleges and universities around the nation are now turning out so many fine young golfers that it is not at all uncommon to hear of collegiate stars making the big jump into the professional ranks. In the past, it took years of apprenticeship on the pro tour before a young man was ready to win his share of the purses. But all that has changed. Thanks to the emphasis on junior and collegiate golf, today's Whiz Kids of the links are giving the veterans plenty of competition.

Whether you play for pay or for exercise, do your best. Aim for a good score—but have fun. Relax.

Former President Dwight D. Eisenhower found golf the best way to relax and escape pressure. Ike never worried about his score. Good or bad, the president had fun. He enjoyed his tours around the green course in the sunshine and fresh air. Often he said, "A round of golf makes me feel like a new man."

Others from the business and entertainment worlds find similar fun and relaxation in golf. Television celebrities like Perry Como and Bing Crosby spend every free moment on the course.

And so do many sports stars. Whitey Ford and Mickey Mantle of the New York Yankees, Kyle Rote and Frank Gifford of the Football Giants and those former Dodger baseball greats

Peewee Reese and Jackie Robinson are among the big-name athletes who consider golf a wonderful way to "get away from it all."

These fellows are all pros—not as golfers—and they always play to win. More importantly, they play to relax and have a good time. They have learned, just as you will learn, the secret of enjoying golf.

Yes, this great game is yours for the taking if you will just remember that *golf can be fun!*

Chapter II

The Mental Approach

Golf is as much mental as physical.

It is a game that must be played with your brains as well as with your body.

Human weaknesses are always present in golf—anger, frustration and impatience. All are your enemies, in golf as in life. You must defeat them just as you conquer the game itself.

Learning to develop the proper temperament toward golf is perhaps the hardest job you face as a young beginner. The right mental outlook is a "must" if you hope to become a good player. The right mental outlook also will help you to enjoy golf.

It would be wise, then, to make up your mind from the start that there are no shortcuts or back-door secrets to golf success. It is a difficult and demanding game that has defied some of the world's greatest athletes—men who had the physical qualities to become good golfers but who lacked the correct mental approach.

As was mentioned in Chapter One, the best way to enjoy golf is not to expect too much of yourself at the start. Golf sometimes takes years of practice—and patience.

In the beginning, you will encounter disappointments. But don't let them get you down. Be ready to accept disappointment as the price of learning. Very few of us are fortunate enough to be natural golfers. We need time, help and encouragement to acquire any skill at all.

It is quite possible that your first few hours on the practice range will be discouraging. You will hit more bad shots than good ones. And you probably will wonder if you ever will be able to hit the ball long and straight.

The thing to do in these situations is to think positively. That is, think about your good shots and forget the bad ones.

You will be better off in the long run if you remember that we are all human. We all make mistakes in judgement and execution almost anywhere—and especially in golf.

This is what makes the game such a great challenge. You never reach the point where you can't improve. Even the top professionals, men who consistently make fine scores, occasionally turn to each other for advice. Like beginners, they sometimes find that their swing breaks down…or that they lose their touch on the putting green. Then they need outside help, as might any beginner, any duffer.

Unlike newcomers, however, the pros don't panic when something goes wrong. They try to avoid open discouragement and emotional outbursts. This is the temperament youngsters must strive to achieve on the road to successful golf.

Bobby Jones once remarked:

"You learn very soon in golf that you can be your own worst enemy. Your ability to win depends on how well you stand up under the pressures brought on by your own mental shortcomings."

Jones spoke from bitter personal experience. As a 14-year-old whiz in Atlanta, Ga., Bobby was frequently subject to outbursts of temper. He threw clubs when he missed a shot. He broke clubs. He stomped. He fumed. He mumbled to himself.

"I kept this up," recalls Jones, "until it dawned on me that the only one I was hurting was myself."

Bobby started winning championships when he accepted the bad shots along with the good ones. As he gained maturity, he learned to control his temper. He put bad shots out of his mind immediately and concentrated on making his next shot a good one.

"I finally had achieved temperamental balance," Jones said years later.

Just what do we mean by temperamental balance? Primarily,

16

it is the ability to keep your emotions in check; not letting them run away with you and spoil your composure—and your golf.

You have achieved a balanced outlook when you can smile after a poor shot and say to yourself, "Okay, I know what I did wrong that time. My next one will make up for it."

There are a great many stylists in golf, players with "picture" swings and wonderful form. But oddly enough, they aren't always the winners of big tournaments. Why? Simply because many of them lack balanced outlooks. Very often the top prizes go to players whose form is not perfect but whose temperament is even and mild and geared to winning golf.

As someone once remarked, "Character shows through on a golf course...win or lose."

Concentration figures in the process of learning golf but many instructors differ on the extent of its importance.

Some, like former champ Byron Nelson, maintain that, "Concentration belongs high on the list of essential considerations. It is necessary to winning golf."

Others state that too much emphasis on concentration is an obstacle to the beginner.

Most agree, however, that a certain amount of concentration

Make every shot with careful planning and mental preparation.

is needed. You concentrate on your schoolwork and on your hobbies. It follows, then, that you also must think about golf and devote time and study to it.

A common fault of some instructors is that they crowd the beginner's mind with so many technical details it is almost impossible for the pupil to think about swinging the club.

The dangers of over-concentration are many. It causes added pressure. It results in a build-up of physical tension. The muscles in the shoulders, arms and hands become taut and stiff. The fingers lose their "feel." The legs are locked. There is little or no flexibility in the body. The result: a swing that is more mechanical than natural.

"Keep the left arm straight...head down...knees flexed... cock the wrists...turn the hips...plant the left foot on the down-swing...follow-through."

These are but a few of the details which beginners are often asked to remember in the split second it takes to swing the club. It is, of course, impossible to do so and still hit the ball.

The fewer instructions the novice has to remember, the better his chances of swinging naturally. The technical details can be considered as the pupil progresses. Try to learn and understand the various parts of the swing—and then put them all together in an easy, natural movement.

Pro Ernest Jones, a great golf instructor, tells a story which illustrates this point.

Jones was having trouble teaching a woman to swing properly. Her mind was crowded with the do's and don'ts of golf. No matter how hard Jones tried, he couldn't convince her to swing naturally.

One day on the practice tee, Jones was having his usual troubles with the lady golfer when he noticed a young caddy swinging a club nearby. He called the boy over, teed up a ball and asked him to hit it.

The young lad obliged and socked the ball 200 yards down the fairway. He did it nonchalantly, almost casually.

The woman blinked in amazement and asked the boy, "What were you thinking about when you hit that ball?"

"Nothing," answered the caddy. "Nothing at all."

"But that's impossible," she blurted. "There are a hundred things you have to remember to hit a ball that well."

"Maybe so, lady," the boy replied, "but I don't think of anything. I just swing."

That convinced the woman she was on the wrong track. Then and there she decided to free her mind of all those unimportant details and concentrate only on swinging the club. Her game improved immediately.

The mental struggle with golf begins the day you step on the course to play your first round. At once you are confronted with obstacles other than your own emotions. You are ready to cope with these problems only if you have learned to balance your temperament.

Perhaps the soundest advice anyone can give you at this stage is to *play within yourself.*

Learn to recognize your own ability and your own faults. After several practice sessions, and maybe a lesson from a qualified pro, you should have a good idea of how far you can hit the ball...which are your best shots...and which clubs you use best.

One of the most important things to remember is not to try and overpower the game. A majority of beginners lack the size and experience to knock the ball a mile. So instead of going for home runs, try for nice, solid singles.

Approach the game slowly. Don't rush things. You have youth on your side. There are many years ahead of you. So, don't attempt to learn everything there is to learn in a few weeks.

If you follow this advice, low scores will come sooner than you think.

Playing golf is much like being a pitcher in baseball. The pitcher thinks carefully before throwing the ball. He studies the batter and decides which pitch will work best. Sometimes he throws a fast ball. Other times he relies on a curve or a slider to fool the batter. But he's always thinking. He never rushes.

It is similar in football when, in a high-pressure situation, the quarterback must think carefully and exercise judgement in calling the next play. A wrong move might mean defeat.

The pressure is on you too every time you select a club. You are like the pitcher or the quarterback thinking about his next move.

Think—and make the right move.

But even if it is the wrong move, the wrong club, don't fret. Every shot in golf is a *new game*.

Lack of careful thinking is a common fault among golfers. Too many weekend players simply walk up to the ball and swing away without taking the trouble to select the right club or look over the situation. In their haste to hit the ball, they forget planning is needed on each and every shot.

Don't fall into this bad habit. You will be surprised at how many strokes you can save by *visualizing each shot before you hit the ball*.

Line up all shots—even a putt.

If you have ever seen pro golfers in action, you know what careful preparations they make before each shot. They stand behind the ball for several seconds, making mental notes on the trouble that lies ahead. They take into account the wind, the condition of the grass, location of sand traps and water hazards. When they finally step up to stroke the ball, they have a clear mental picture of what they should do, and what is likely to happen when they do it. They leave as little to chance as possible.

Of course, such preparation is too involved for most youngsters. But it doesn't hurt to start learning how to *think golf* as well as play it.

Here are a few simple reminders that will help you, the beginner, to save strokes:

1. Never be in a hurry. Walk fast between shots but take your time planning the next one.

2. Don't take chances. It doesn't pay to gamble.

3. Play the easiest and safest shot at all times.

4. Avoid trying to "kill" the ball. Play with your brains as well as with your brawn. A soft, easy swing will be better for you.

5. Select your club carefully.

6. When approaching the green, play for the largest part of it instead of shooting right at the hole. Play it safe. Just make the green, and then worry about the hole.

7. When putting, be sure to "read" the green. That is, size up your putt from behind, noting such things as distance to the cup, the break of the green, the texture of the grass—is it short enough to allow the ball to roll fast, or is it so heavy the ball will be slowed down?

Follow these tips and you'll find winning golf comes a lot easier.

As Tommy Armour, another of the great teaching pros, says:

"Each golf course is so designed as to reward the smart golfer and penalize a foolish one."

You will be getting off on the right foot in golf if you remember to *use your own head as well as the clubhead!*

Chapter III

The Grip

People are often advised to "get a grip on yourself."

In golf, one of the first lessons to be learned is to get a grip—on your club. You must hold the club before you do anything else, and how you hold it is all-important.

Golf professionals have advanced several different theories on how a golf club should be held. Some prefer the Vardon or overlapping grip. Some teach the interlocking method. Others lean to the baseball grip. But on one basic fact the experts are in complete agreement:

A sound grip is the only way to a sound swing!

Unfortunately, many beginners do not share this view. In their haste to get on with the business of hitting the ball, novices often overlook the vital role played by the hands. They think the grip will take care of itself. Avoid this mistaken belief at all costs.

Gripping the club is the very first phase of the swing. The grip must be correct or everything else that follows will be wrong.

For this reason, the grip will be treated in detail in this early chapter. As the old saying goes: We must learn to walk before we run.

Before going into technical descriptions of the three basic grips (Vardon, interlocking and baseball), let's consider the grip in general terms.

To begin with, your fingers and hands are your only link with the clubhead—and it is the clubhead which strikes the ball. You can see from this one fact alone why it is so important that you form this connecting link with great care.

22

Fingers exert a gentle pressure so that you get the "feel" of the swing.

The relation of the hands to the club might be compared to the electrical wiring in your home. If something goes wrong with the electric wires, the current cannot perform its role of lighting the house.

In golf, your hands are the wires through which the power generated by your body is conducted down the shaft and into the clubhead. A poor or faulty connection can short-circuit your entire swing.

To further illustrate this build-up of power, let's picture a game of "snap the whip" which you probably have played at one time or another on ice skates. In this game, ten or fifteen skaters hook their arms and start moving in a huge circle. The inner, or anchor, end of the line hardly moves but the outer, or whip, end keeps picking up speed. Soon, the end man is traveling five or six times as fast as the other skaters.

Now let's suppose that two skaters in the middle of the whip suddenly unhooked their arms. What do you think would happen? Speed and power would no longer be transferred from one skater to another, and the whipping movement at the end of the line would be lost. The connecting link would be broken.

This is similar to what happens in a golf swing if your hands do not form a perfect connection with the shaft of the club. The power generated in your body is lost somewhere along the line. It never reaches the clubhead—the "whip" end of the your swing.

To achieve a sound swing, the hands must work together. They must be a unit throughout the swing, neither hand dominating the action more than the other. Two hands are better than one, the saying goes. This holds true in golf, however, *only* if both hands are used in perfect unison.

When executing a golf stroke, the clubface must be "square to the ball"—that is, at right angles to the intended line of flight—

at the instant of impact. And the only way to accomplish this is through a good grip with the hands operating together.

If either hand, or both, are placed too far to the left or right, then the clubface, instead of being "square to the ball," also will be turned to one side. Result: the ball will not travel a straight course. It will be "off line," as the golfers say.

This is why it is so important to make *both hands function as one* from start to finish of the swing.

The exact positioning of the left and right hands will be discussed shortly. Right here, though, suppose we take a look at the general alignment of the hands—no matter which grip you may use.

We will start with the left because this is the upper hand, the one which most golfers place on the shaft first when forming their grip.

The back of the left hand should always face the direction in which you intend to hit.

During the swing, the action of the left hand is similar to that of a backhand tennis stroke. Picture a tennis player hitting a backhand return and you will have a good idea of what your left hand should be doing in a golf swing.

In golfing terminology, this is known as *hitting with the back of the hand*.

The palm of the right hand always faces in the direction you intend hitting the ball. Thus, the right hand is placed *behind* the shaft of the club, a position opposite that of the left hand. The action of the right hand is similar to a forehand swing in tennis.

Or, to try another illustration, its action is like that used when you throw a softball underhand.

Repeating the general function of the hands:

With the left hand, the stroke is always *backhand*. The right hand action is always *forehand*.

Now for the next general problem of the grip—how tight should you hold the club?

Here's how both hands look on shaft before grip is taken—back of left hand and palm of right hand face direction of the shot.

Too tight a grip tends to restrict the natural movement of your wrists and arms. A very loose grip will break down during the course of the swing. You must seek a happy medium: not too tight; not too loose.

The grip must be firm but not vise-like. The hands should be in complete control of the club at all times and yet not overpower it.

One of the most common mistakes among beginners is their tendency to grasp the shaft of the club as if they intended to strangle it. Their fingers are rigid, their knuckles stiff, their arm muscles knotted. A free, easy swing is impossible. They are lucky, indeed, to just hit the ball.

As an example of what these common errors can do to you, close your hands and squeeze as hard as you can. Notice how tight your fingers feel, and also how your wrist and forearm stiffen. This is how a tense grip ties you up while you are attempting to swing the golf club.

On the other hand, if you take hold of the club too loosely, you cannot hope to control it throughout the swing. With a wishy-washy grip, you may find the club turns in your hands at critical points of the stroke—at the top of the backswing or, worse yet, at the instant the clubhead meets the ball.

As was mentioned earlier, you should strive for a grip that is a compromise between the so-called "death hold" and the too-casual grip.

The complete grip. Hands and fingers exert firm and gentle pressure.

The ideal is a firm grip. The hands are always in control. They exert pressure, but it is *gentle* and *controlled*. The hands also have flexibility, however, permitting a free, easy and natural swing.

The great Walter Hagen, who shared the golfing headlines with Bobby Jones, had such a grip. Ben Hogan described it by saying, "It is beautiful . . . delicate and at the same time powerful."

Of the three basic grips mentioned in this chapter, the Vardon grip—also called the overlapping grip—is more widely used and taught than either the interlocking or the baseball grips.

This is because most experts agree that the Vardon grip, originated by Harry Vardon almost a century ago, best promotes what top golfers strive for—complete unison between the hands.

With the help of the accompanying photographs, let's take a closer look at the exact positioning of the hands in the Vardon grip.

LEFT HAND: Hold the left hand open and lay the shaft of the club diagonally across the palm from the base of the index finger to the heel of the hand. Now, without changing the posi-

Left hand grip prior to closing fingers on shaft of club.

tion of the club, simply close your fingers around the shaft. If you do this naturally, the thumb will lie straight along the top of the shaft. This left hand grip is known as a *palm and finger grip* since both parts of the hand help to control the club.

RIGHT HAND: The right hand grip is essentially a *finger grip* because the club is held more in the fingers than with the palm. This provides better "feel." In taking the right hand grip, lay

Finger control is key to the right hand position.

the shaft across the last joint of all four fingers. Most of the pressure in the right hand grip is supplied by the middle two fingers. You must be careful to avoid exerting too much pressure with the thumb and index finger.

The thing which distinguishes the Vardon grip from all other methods of holding a golf club is the position of the little finger (pinky) of the right hand.

In closing the fingers of the right hand around the shaft, the little finger overlaps the left hand, and fits into the groove formed by the index and middle fingers of the left hand. The position of the little finger is what leads golfers to refer to the Vardon grip as "overlapping."

Vardon grip, front view. Vardon grip from side.

After closing the fingers of the right hand and placing the pinky in its overlapping groove on the left hand, you complete the right hand grip by positioning the thumb slightly to the left side of the shaft.

Next, let's examine the *interlocking grip*.

This grip is the same, basically, as the Vardon grip. The difference is that the pinky of the right hand, instead of overlapping as in the Vardon method, interlocks with the index finger of the left hand. This sounds complicated, but it isn't. The advantage of this grip is that it provides an aid for people whose hands are too small to overlap as in the Vardon grip. The interlocking position makes it easier for them to maintain a firm grip on the shaft.

To make the interlocking grip work as effectively as the Vardon, keep in mind the basic fact that both hands still must function as a unit. Another point to remember is that the left hand is a *finger and palm* grip while the right hand is a *finger* grip.

Two views of the basic interlocking grip.

The *baseball grip* is the most natural way to hold a club, and probably the best for new or young golfers. Good weekend players and many top professionals, including Art Wall, Jr. and Bob Rosburg, also use the baseball grip with winning results.

31

Those who favor the baseball grip like its simplicity. The baseball grip is a *ten-finger grip*. All fingers of both hands are placed on the shaft. The left hand position is exactly the same as in the Vardon and interlocking grips. The right hand does not overlap or interlock. You grip the club almost the same way you would hold a baseball bat.

What advantages does the baseball grip offer the young golfer?

First, because it is the natural way to hold a club, it gives beginners a better "feel" of the swing. Since the little finger of the right hand is in a comfortable position, the baseball grip does not build up tension in the right hand at address. The Vardon grip often does. The wrists are looser and more flexible, and thus it is a simple matter to begin a free and easy backswing.

And just as important is the fact that the beginner is not mentally burdened with intricate details of the other grips. The

Close-up views of baseball grip.

thing to keep in mind is that, like other methods, the baseball grip features finger and palm control by the left hand and strictly finger control by the right.

32

If you remember this basic principle, you should be able to get just as good results with the baseball grip as with the others.

As a beginner, *try the baseball grip first*.

Bob Rosburg, who has won fame and wealth on the pro golf tour, defends his use of the baseball grip by saying, ". . . because all the fingers are on the shaft of the club, the baseball grip gives feel. This makes those delicate short shots that much easier."

"The baseball swing gives firmness and power," adds Art Wall, Jr., another top money-winner among the pros.

Rosburg and Wall are the only two outstanding professionals who swing with the baseball grip. But many others have confessed that they would start with this grip if they had it to do over again.

Once you decide which grip is for you, practice it as much as you can. Daily practice, either in your room or in the backyard, will give you the "feel" of the grip. Before you know it, the grip will become almost automatic. Every time you hold a club, your fingers will naturally fall into the proper alignment. It will be like holding your fork at the dinner table or your toothbrush in the morning. You won't even have to think about it.

When you have mastered the knack of picking up a club with "feel" and confidence, you are ready to start shooting for par scores.

Chapter IV

Addressing the Ball

In all forms of athletics, good footwork is vital to winning performance. Golf is no exception.

The act of preparing yourself to hit a golf ball is known as *addressing the ball,* and is so important that it must be mentioned here before we move on to such matters as how to swing the club.

The success of each and every shot is determined by the preparations you make *before* swinging the club. You must set the stage if you hope to get good results.

There is no such thing as simply walking up to the ball and swinging away. Golf is easy—but not that easy.

As in the grip (which we discussed in the last chapter), addressing the ball calls for strict attention to several details which will help insure best results.

The first of these is the stance—the position of the feet in relation to your body and to the ball.

Good posture is the best way to good shots. Relaxed stance is essential.

The stance is just as important as the grip because it places you in the final position prior to actually striking the ball. After taking your stance, also known as "standing up to the ball," there is no second chance . . . no time to change. You are committed to the shot—for better or for worse.

You may not realize it, but an error of two or three inches in your stance can result in an error of 50 or 60 yards in the flight of the golf ball.

Thus, the importance of a sound basic starting position cannot be over-emphasized.

Assuming the proper stance might be compared to setting your alarm clock before going to bed. You check the time, adjust the dial and set the alarm button for a certain hour. You have made the necessary preparations. The clock does the rest.

So it is with the stance. You set things up so that the final result—the act of swinging the club—comes off as planned.

Your alarm clock won't go off if you don't make the necessary arrangements ahead of time. Similarly, your swing won't give the desired results unless you arrange details beforehand.

There are several parts of the golf stance: position of the feet, knees, arms, upper body and head.

Since, as pro Tommy Armour says, "Athletes are built from the ground up," let's first consider the role played by the feet.

There are three basic foot positions:

Square, open and *closed.*

Of these, the square stance is the most common. It, in the opinion of many instructors, provides the best feeling of balance during the swing.

In the square stance, the toes of both feet are square to, or touching, a line which is parallel to the intended line of flight of the ball. You can get a better picture of the square position by laying a golf club at your feet while addressing the ball. With the club pointed in the direction of the shot, your toes should touch it. Sometimes the left toe may be pointed slightly outward, but the stance is still regarded as being square.

Square stance, front view.   Square stance, side view.

Using the same club as a guide for your feet, let's now look at the open stance. In this stance, your right foot is still touching the club. But the left foot has been drawn back several inches, creating the "open" position.

Open stance with left foot drawn back.

The closed stance finds the right foot drawn back from the guide line while the left foot, unlike the open stance, is square to the line.

In closed stance, right foot is drawn back.

Each of the above-mentioned foot positions has its own special use, which will be discussed later.

Right now, though, let us consider another important part of the stance: How far apart should the feet be?

The ideal position is to have the feet as far apart as the width of your shoulders. This promotes maximum balance and freedom of body movement during the swing.

Actually there is no iron-clad rule about the spread of the feet as long as they are not too close together—or too far apart. You should stand so as to achieve balance and comfort. Foot placement often varies with a person's height and weight. It shouldn't take you long to determine just what the right spacing is for your particular needs. Better still, if you are fortunate enough to be taking lessons from a pro, he will watch your swing and advise you how to stand when addressing the ball.

Feet should be spaced about as wide as shoulders.

A stance which is excessively wide locks the body and restricts the swing. The narrow stance often results in lack of balance and co-ordination.

As you progress in golf, you will find that the spacing of the feet can be changed to meet certain situations—close together for short iron shots, wide for tee shots, etc.

At present, however, concentrate on a stance that will give you a solid base and enough flexibility to swing freely. Strive for comfort.

In discussing correct address posture, you also must consider the knees.

The knees act as springs or shock absorbers for the body during the swing. They should be bent slightly as you address the ball. This flexing of the knee joints puts you into a comfortable position and helps to lessen tension.

This bending action of the knees is often referred to as "sitting down on the ball" because, as you bend the knees, you resemble a person preparing to sit in a chair.

Bend knees to "sit down" on ball.

Now for the arms . . .

The best word to use in describing the ideal position of the arms while addressing the ball is *natural*. Let your arms hang loosely and relaxed at your side. After gripping the club, reach naturally for the ball. Do not stand so far from the ball that you must stretch for it. Nor should you stand too close. Exactly how far you stand from the ball, of course, will be determined by your height and the length of your arms. It will help your swing, too, if the elbows are kept as close to the body as possible.

At address, arms hang naturally and in a relaxed position. Upper body is relaxed and head is fixed over the ball.

The upper body must be erect but relaxed. Don't attempt to lower your body by bending at the waist. You achieve the lowering effect by flexing your knees. Too many golfers bend over at the waist while their knees remain rigid and locked. This is wrong.

In taking your stance, remember that your head must stay in a fixed position during most of the swing. The head does not remain stationary all the time, of course. It will rise with the natural movement of your body and shoulders as you follow-through. But it is vitally important to hold your head still until the ball has been struck. Lifting the head too soon and taking your eye off the ball results in all sorts of miseries.

Before moving on to the other phases of the address, let's quickly review the major points just outlined:

1. Feet spaced comfortably (shoulder width) no matter which of the three stances (open, closed or square) that you use.

2. Knees flexed slightly to put you in a comfortable, relaxed position over the ball.

3. Arms hanging naturally at sides with elbows close to the body.

4. Back erect but relaxed.

5. Eyes on the ball; head stationary.

The success, or failure, of your shot depends on the completeness and detail of your preparation. Striking the ball is merely the last part of a chain reaction.

Where does this chain reaction start?

Well, it begins the moment you take a club from your bag. The first thing to do is place your hands around the shaft of the club and check every point of your grip—finger and palm control with the left hand, finger control with the right, and the feeling that both hands are ready to work as a unit. To check the grip further, take a couple of easy practice swings. If your hands are out of alignment, you will sense it instantly. Then you make the necessary adjustments.

Next, examine the face of your club to make sure it is square to the line of flight—in other words, directly facing the hole. Your grip won't help at all if the clubface is at an angle that may produce a poor shot.

Step No. 3 involves getting a mental picture of the hole you are playing. This gives you the opportunity to take note of such things as trees, sand traps, water hazards, etc. With these factors in mind, you have an idea of where and how you must hit the ball.

Many complete their mental picture by standing directly over or behind the ball and studying the situation.

The danger point in preparing for the shot comes when you address the ball. This is when you are apt to feel the pressure of the game. It is at this point that some golfers "freeze." Muscle tension builds up. Hands and legs become rigid. The swing that follows is stiff and unnatural.

What can you do to avoid this tension or "freeze?"

For one thing, you can use a "waggle"—an easy, relaxed movement of the clubhead behind the ball just before starting the full swing. In the "waggle," you move the club back

To avoid muscle tension and stiffness, don't address ball until you are loose and relaxed.

and forth several inches to help break down tension in the hands, arms and legs.

You probably have seen the equivalent of the "waggle" in other sports—a pitcher kicking the rubber prior to starting his wind-up; a batter swishing his bat as he awaits the pitch; a basketball player bouncing the ball on the floor several times before taking a foul shot; a boxer dancing in his corner before the opening bell.

Like the "waggle" in golf, these preliminary movements by athletes in other sports serve the same purpose—to loosen the muscles and relax the mind.

The "waggle" also carries the clubhead part way along the path it will travel when you actually swing. Ben Hogan compares the "waggle" to a "miniature practice swing."

There are, naturally, many different methods of "waggling." It depends on individuals and temperament. Some players need more of a "waggle" than others to get them loosened up. It won't take you long to find out how much of a preliminary movement you require to feel relaxed and ready to swing.

Some golfers don't use the "waggle." But they all have some kind of a trick to avoid tension as they address the ball.

Julius Boros, a ranking pro player, says:

"If you don't 'waggle,' at least stay in motion one way or another. Keep some part of your body moving—knees, hands, arms or feet."

Before you move on to the next chapter, it might be well to re-trace your steps and review our discussions of the grip and stance. Only a firm and unified grip, and a comfortable, relaxed stance will enable you to master the sound golf swing.

Chapter V

The Swing's the Thing

The game of golf has one basic objective—striking the ball with the club.

Everything else that happens is incidental to this single act.

The right mental attitude...the grip...the stance. All of these are merely preliminary to your real reason for playing the game—swinging the club so that it meets the ball satisfactorily.

In the words of pro Ernest Jones, "It is the swing, and only the swing, which makes the golfer."

You can't hit the golf ball without swinging. Thus, learning to swing correctly is an immediate requirement. Perhaps "learning" is the wrong word. No one can learn the golf swing overnight, or by reading a book. But at least this discussion of the swing should help to put you on the right track, help you to avoid common mistakes which plague the average golfer.

The lessons on the grip and stance have prepared you for the project at hand.

Now . . . for the swing!

What is the swing anyway? How would you describe it?

Webster's Dictionary tells us that swing is ". . . movement to and fro . . . a flourish or a sweep . . . a motion like that of a pendulum."

Very proper definitions, to be sure. But they don't quite answer our question. Why? Probably because a golf swing cannot be described in words alone. It must be *felt!*

There is something about a sound, properly-executed golf swing that immediately communicates itself to the swinger.

44

If he swings and hits the ball correctly, he knows it—he feels good all over. It is a sensation that seems to start at the moment the club hits the ball. The feeling extends up the shaft and into the player's hands and arms.

The reverse is also true. When you dub a shot, you know that immediately, too. You don't have to wait to see your ball dribble off the tee.

Swinging the clubhead at the golf ball is fundamentally a simple and natural process. But at the same time, it is a technique which contains numerous booby-traps for the unwary student of the game.

In golf, it often seems easier to do things the wrong way. But in this game the result of doing things incorrectly, especially when swinging the club, is discouragement and frustration.

As was mentioned earlier, there are no short-cuts to golf. But understanding the principles of the swing certainly will make learning the game much easier and more pleasant.

For our purposes, we will divide the golf swing into three separate parts:

The backswing—The act of sweeping the club up and away from the ball at the very beginning of the stroke.

The downswing—The act of bringing the club down and hitting the ball.

The follow-through—Finishing the stroke after striking the ball.

The golf swing, as viewed by the human eye, is anything but a three-part movement. Correctly done, it is one, smooth, fluid action of the hands, arms and body. Nevertheless, each of these three movements contributes to the overall rhythm and effectiveness of the swing.

Since the stroke is started by taking the clubhead away from the ball, let's begin with the backswing.

First, and perhaps most important, never begin your backswing until you have carefully reviewed and checked your grip, stance and posture. You can't expect to swing properly if there is a weakness in either your grip or your stance. These are the foundation stones upon which you build a good swing.

Remember, too, that learning to relax as you address the ball helps your swing. If you feel tight or tense, then by all means step away from the ball before starting your backswing. Take a deep breath. Shake the tenseness out of your hands and arms. You probably have seen pitchers and batters do this all the time in tight baseball games.

Now you are relaxed. So, with grip firm...stance correct... posture comfortable, you can start your backswing.

The backswing is vital because it sets the tempo for the entire swing. In other words, a hurried backswing will result in a hurried shot. The rhythm established by the first movement of the club will determine the rhythm and timing of the entire swing.

The initial movement of the clubhead away from the ball should be made *slowly*. Don't hurry.

Although both hands are on the shaft of the club, try to start your backswing with the left hand doing most of the work. Left hand control keeps the club low to the ground, which is very important. Left hand control also prevents the clubface from turning.

To learn this move, hold the club with only your left hand

and practice swinging it back slowly and smoothly parallel to the ground. Soon you will develop strength in your left hand, and you will be able to start your backswing properly.

A good trick to help you keep the club low on your backswing is to stick a tee in the ground eight or ten inches directly behind the ball. As you take the clubhead back, make an effort to brush this tee. This will tell you whether or not you are keeping the club in the proper groove. Do this and you also will avoid one of the most serious mistakes made by beginners —starting the backswing by picking the club up with the right hand.

If you start the clubhead back with firm left hand control, the natural turning of your arms, shoulders and hips will get the club to its correct position at the top of the swing. In other words, you don't have to rush things by lifting the club with the right hand. *Let the left hand begin the backswing.*

There are many different movements in the golf swing. The backswing, alone, for instance, has four parts. Gradually coming into play in this order are:

1. The hands, particularly the left hand, start the backswing.

2. Then the arms join the backward motion.

3. Halfway through the backswing, the shoulders begin turning to the right.

4. Finally, the hips turn to the right as the backswing reaches its highest point.

The beginner, however, should not think of the backswing in its separate parts. Rather, he should consider it as a single, smooth action of hands and arms that automatically puts his club into the right position to begin the downswing.

The more mechanical you are in swinging—that is, if you *do* consider its separate parts—the more difficult it will be to learn a proper backswing. Concentrate on being free and easy, and learning the "feel" of a smooth, one-piece movement.

One final note on the backswing. Beginners sometimes find it easier to start with a *short, compact backswing*. As a newcomer, don't try and take a full wind-up like a Sammy Snead preparing to lash at the ball. A short backswing enables you to control the club more effectively and keep the clubhead in its proper groove. A long, looping backswing such as the pros use often collapses at the top. The club wobbles in your hands, and you hit a poor shot. Get the "feel" of a short backswing first—and then you can lengthen your swing arc.

The danger point in the golf swing is at the top. This is the crucial area. This is where your backswing becomes the downswing; where your swing changes direction and starts its downward sweep toward the ball.

Most flaws in the swing can be traced to errors originating at the top.

Perhaps the most common mistake is made by golfers who are impatient to start down. They can hardly wait to "murder" the ball. This is known as "hitting from the top"—that is, be-

Pause at top of backswing is important.

ginning your downswing before you have even completed the backswing.

To avoid this error, you should strive for a *pause at the top of the swing.*

This is not a long pause. Rather it is a split-second hesitation that enables you to get set before starting back down toward the ball.

We have compared the golf swing to the motion of a pendulum on a grandfather's clock. The pendulum swings one way at a certain speed and rhythm—and back again at the same speed and rhythm. It doesn't hurry back.

The same might be said of the golf swing. The tempo should be basically the same one way as it is the other, even though you do generate more speed at the point of impact than you do when taking the club away from the ball.

49

Downswing action is just the reverse of backswing movement. As you reach the top of the swing and prepare to start the downswing, the action is triggered by the hips turning back toward the ball. Then the shoulders get into the swing. The arms follow. Finally the hands, which must delay their hitting action until they reach belt level, complete the downward movement.

On the downswing, Ben Hogan says, "Keep any conscious hand effort out of the swing until the arms move down to hip level."

Hitting area comes at belt level.

You should be able to get your downswing moving in good fashion if you remember this: *the hips are the key*. Turning them into the downswing action *first* practically pulls all other parts of the body into proper and effective alignment.

What happens to your body's weight during the backswing and the downswing?

At address, the weight is evenly balanced. As the backswing begins, the weight shifts slightly onto the right foot. It stays here until the downswing begins. As the hips, shoulders and arms start toward the ball on the downswing, the weight is transferred back to the left foot—where most of it should be at impact.

A warning note about the distribution of weight: don't make a mechanical effort to transfer your weight on either the backswing or downswing. Just swing naturally. In most cases, the weight transfer will take care of itself—especially if you have been careful in assuming the correct stance when addressing the ball.

Now we come to the final part of the golf swing, the *follow-through*.

What is the follow-through? Anybody can follow through, but it is difficult to put into words. Shall we say that it is the completion of the natural arc of the swing. You achieve a good follow-through by smoothly co-ordinating all parts of the body involved in striking the ball.

When hitting a ball, a golfer can hardly avoid some kind of follow-through. He can't swing merely until he hits the ball and then stop short.

Yet, many golfers feel their role in the swing is completed when they hit the ball. How wrong they are!

The action of your clubhead, hands and body *after* hitting the ball is very important to the success of the shot. A good follow-through is proof of a sound swing. When you swing correctly, the follow-through usually will be correct. A faulty swing, however, leads to an incomplete follow-through.

The follow-through is not unique to golf alone. Most other sports call for follow-throughs of some type to assure proper executions.

Start backswing in one piece with left hand in control.

Wrists and arms are still straight as club is taken back

Head fixed on ball, left arm straight at top of backswing. Weight on right foot.

Pause at the top prior to unwinding into downswing.

Weight shifts to left foot as hands near hitting area on downswing.

Hands finish high on the follow-through.

A batter in baseball wouldn't think of checking the swing of his bat just as he meets the ball. He knows he will get added power and distance by whipping his bat in a circle to complete his swing. In tennis, too, you must follow-through, forehand or backhand, to obtain consistent stroking.

To execute a good follow-through, make an effort to keep the clubface square at impact and swing the clubhead straight out along the intended line of flight. Avoid rolling your wrists to the left. Keep them in line, too. And don't collapse your grip as you feel the clubhead meet the ball.

You can practice your follow-through by placing a tee in the ground eight or ten inches ahead of your ball and slightly to the right, and then attempting to hit it with your clubhead as you finish the stroke. It is hard to do. But just trying it will make you conscious of keeping your clubhead straight along the line of flight.

Concentrating on a solid follow-through also will help you to achieve greater clubhead speed on your downswing. If you are thinking in terms of finishing strong, then it's a good bet that you will really whip your clubhead into the ball with good speed at impact.

It bears repeating that the principles of the swing covered in this chapter are perhaps the most important lessons a beginner must learn. So, don't be afraid to go back and re-read. You must have a clear understanding of the golf swing before moving on. Always remember:

The swing's the thing!

Chapter VI

Hitting the Woods

Like the home run in baseball, there is nothing in golf to compare with a long, booming drive.

Socking a ball 200 yards or more off the tee with a driver (No. 1 wood) gives the average golfer a thrill that makes him forget the many bad shots he hits.

The driver is the heavy artillery in your golf arsenal. It is the longest club. It is the heaviest club. It gives you the greatest distance—if you hit it correctly.

Other woods, such as the No. 2, 3, 4 and 5 woods, also are distance clubs. But they are designed primarily for playing the ball off the fairway—that is, without the ball being teed up.

The driver can be your best friend or your worst enemy. It can make the game easy, or it can get you into trouble. It all depends on your mental approach to hitting the ball off the tee.

Nine out of ten golfers make trouble for themselves with the driver by swinging too hard and too fast.

As they address the ball before a tee shot, some sort of golfing gremlin seems to whisper:

"You're really going to murder this one . . . you'll knock it a country mile. Go ahead, pal, slug away."

These same golfers, when using any other club in the bag, will swing slowly and rhythmically, the way they are supposed to. But put a driver in their hands and they immediately become power-mad sluggers. They think they can substitute muscle for timing. But they can't.

In listening to that mischievous gremlin, many players become tense. They disregard rhythm and inject an overdose of power in the swing. The result: a missed shot, either scuffed or topped, and always badly off line.

What causes the average weekend player to try and tear the cover off the ball with a No. 1 wood? No one really seems to know. But most instructors agree it is a problem that must be solved by beginners and experts alike.

Some of the longest hitters in golf admit that the only way to stroke a good tee shot with a driver is by swinging easily and smoothly, and by suppressing the inner desire to overpower the ball.

George Bayer, the six-foot, six-inch 245-pound giant who has hit tee shots of better than 375 yards, says:

"Don't swing too hard. Slugging makes you exceed your natural swing . . . and the distance you get will not make up for the loss of timing. And timing is everything in golf."

As Bayer points out, when you seek extra power you automatically inject added leverage into the stroke, leverage that can ruin your rhythm and timing.

Former driving champion Jimmy Thompson insists that balance is all-important to successful wood shots. "If you lose the balance," says Jimmy, "you also lose the shot."

Balance . . . timing . . . rhythm. These are the ingredients you need for long, accurate tee shots. Power won't help unless it is applied in the proper place—in those last few inches before the clubhead meets the ball.

There is no percentage in trying to belt the ball out of sight merely because you happen to have a driver in your hands. Think in terms of letting the clubhead do the work. You will be surprised to find that distance comes almost automatically. Accuracy too.

This is why some women golfers get almost as much distance as many male players. They lack the size and strength of men, but they have learned the secret of achieving maximum speed on the downswing and then letting the clubhead

Women and girls get distance off tee through timing and rhythm.

act as their "muscle."

Right now, though, don't worry about distance. Your first job is to get accuracy with your driver. Groove your swing. Keep the ball in play. Distance will come later.

The "home run" ball is nice to hit. But it can penalize you if it lands in the rough or sails over a nearby fence. The base-ball player who hits a foul home run gets another chance. In golf, however, you get only one chance off the tee—and it had better be good.

The lesson to learn here is that distance lies in timing . . . not in brute strength.

As long as you play the game of golf, you must be prepared to fight this battle with yourself. Your natural instincts tell you to "murder" the ball. But common sense must win out if you hope to become a good golfer.

So much for the psychological aspects of the tee shot. How is the shot actually hit?

The drive gives you one advantage that is present in no other golf shot. You are allowed to tee the ball up on a small wooden peg. You may place it at any spot in the ground (between the tee markers) that you wish. And at any height that you wish.

The face of the driver is perfectly straight. It does not have the upward angle of the other woods. Thus, the beginner sometimes encounters difficulty getting his tee shot into the air.

To overcome this problem, start by teeing your ball high enough to insure that the clubhead has plenty of room to get under it and send it in an upward direction. Later on you can tee the ball lower as your swing with the driver becomes more grooved. But for the time being, tee the ball high. You will get better results.

The worst thing you can do is to make a conscious effort to lift the ball with the driver. This can lead only to a topped shot or, worse yet, a complete miss.

If your swing is sound, *the clubhead will do the work*. And this includes getting the ball into the air.

When addressing the ball on the tee, take your regular stance with feet spaced about as wide as the shoulders—or maybe a fraction wider. Then play the ball off your left foot; that is, at a point opposite your left toe.

This positioning of the ball is very important in the drive. In most other shots, the ball is played toward the middle of your feet so you can strike it with a downward blow of the clubhead. The driver, however, should be hit slightly on the upswing. Perhaps *sweep* is a better word.

Because the ball is played off your left foot in the drive, you must make an extra effort to stay down and hit through the shot. Any lifting of the head, arms or shoulders will result in the clubhead just grazing the top of the ball. *Stay with the shot!*

It would be well at this point to go back and review the chapter dealing with the backswing. There is an important lesson to remember: take the clubhead back close to the ground as you start the backswing. And take it back slowly.

Keeping the clubhead close to the ground as you begin your swing makes it easier for you to bring the club on a low arc as you come back down into the ball. You hit the ball at the lowest point of your swing, or maybe a little on the upswing. And hitting on the upswing gets the ball into the air.

By following these hints, you may avoid one of the most common of all golf errors—topping the ball.

Topping is just what its name implies. Your clubhead merely grazes the top half of the ball instead of hitting it squarely. This causes a shot that never gets into the air. It bounces along the ground—usually not very far.

What causes a topped shot?

Lifting your head before you have hit the ball is probably the biggest reason. If your head comes up too soon and you take your eye off the ball, it is almost certain you won't catch it solidly with the clubface.

Topped shots also are the result of not "hitting through" the ball. Think in terms of staying with the shot—not quitting the instant you make contact—and you will find that topped shots are few and far between.

Next to topping, one of the biggest headaches for beginners and weekend players is slicing. By that we mean hitting the ball a glancing blow that causes it to sail, or spin, far off to the right. A ball slices because it is struck with a clubface that is not square to the line of flight. This gives the ball a clockwise spinning motion that makes it curve to the right.

There are many reasons for slicing. And there are just as many cures. Your best bet, however, is to review again the lessons on grip, stance and posture, and the swing.

Instead of trying to compensate for a slice, as many erroneously do, concentrate instead on *building a sound swing.*

Whenever you top a ball or hit a slice, it is likely you have neglected one or more of the fundamental steps in the golf swing. When this happens, don't resort to trick cures or short-cuts. Instead, go back and review your swing—from the moment you took your grip on the club until the ball was hit. Somewhere you went wrong. Find the weak link in the swing, and you will be back on line in no time.

This advice holds true for the other woods in your bag as well as for the driver. Let's take a look at these clubs.

The brassie (No. 2 wood)—Like all clubs with the exception of the driver, the No. 2 wood is used to hit shots off the fairway. Since you are not permitted to tee up a ball in the fairway, the No. 2 has an angled clubface that is designed to help get the ball into the air. The No. 2 is closest to the driver in length and weight but it is a difficult club to use. Beginners should stay away from this club until they have considerable experience. If you do use the No. 2 wood, try using it off the tee instead of your driver. The angled clubface will insure you getting the ball into air.

The spoon (No. 3 wood)—The spoon is a shorter and lighter club than either the driver or the brassie. It has a more lofted clubface which sends the ball in a higher arc. This club, like the brassie, is often used by women and youngsters when teeing off because it is lighter and easier to control than the driver. It also is a valuable club on "close" fairway lies—where the ball is in a gully, a divot, or partially covered by grass. Learn to use the No. 3 wood. It can be a good friend in many different situations.

The No. 4 wood—This club is even shorter and lighter than the others and has a deeper loft angle to the clubface. Because of this, the No. 4 wood can be used to lift the ball over such obstacles as trees, shrubs, water hazards and hills. Like the spoon, it is ideally suited to fairway situations where you do not have a clean shot at the ball. The No. 4 goes right down into trouble and digs the ball out for you.

The lofted fairway woods have become so popular in recent years that many sets of golf clubs now come with a driver, spoon, No. 4 and No. 5 woods—leaving out the hard-to-use No. 2.

No matter which fairway wood you are swinging, though, the only right way to do it is by *hitting down on the ball!*

This, you may note, is exactly opposite of what we said about the driver. With the driver, you want to hit the ball on the upswing—sweep it off the tee as the clubhead starts upward. This is necessary because the driver has no loft to the clubface, and the ball must be hit on the way up to get any height on it.

With the fairway clubs, however, you should strike the ball a descending blow. By "hitting down" on the ball with either the No. 3 or No. 4 wood, the sharply-angled clubface will send the ball sharply into the air as it leaves the ground.

Exactly what is "hitting down" on the ball? Is it as complicated as it sounds? The answer is "no."

All that is involved is striking the ball a split second before the clubhead reaches the lowest point in the swing. When this happens, the ball is propelled into the air immediately and the clubhead then bites into the ground, taking out a small strip of turf. These strips are called *divots*. The important thing to remember about divots is that they are taken by the clubhead *after* the ball has been struck—not before.

Generally, the fairway woods call for a normal stance with the ball played back toward the middle of your stance. Playing the ball back farther than with the driver enables you to strike it on the way down.

You will find, too, that you must stand closer to the ball with the fairway woods because they are slightly shorter than the driver. In the beginning, it might even be wise to choke up on your No. 3 or No. 4 wood for better control of the club during the swing. A shorter backswing will help, too.

Knowing *when* to use your fairway woods is almost as important as knowing *how* to use them.

Inexperienced golfers should never use a fairway wood if there is even the slightest doubt that they can hit the ball well and cleanly enough to get it into the air. Remember—it doesn't pay to take silly chances. Gambling is for the experts. For your part, *play it safe!*

Hitting a good wood shot is difficult enough under ideal conditions. So, if you decide to use a fairway wood when your ball is in the rough or in a divot hole, keep in mind that *the more difficult the lie, the easier the swing.*

This is another way of saying that you should not attempt to force the ball out of trouble with a wood. The clubhead has been designed to get through to the ball and lift it into the air. You will only spoil things if you try to help the clubhead get that job done.

Use a No. 3 or No. 4 wood only when you have complete confidence that you can hit a good shot. If you aren't sure, go to an iron club.

And speaking of irons . . .

Chapter VII

Ironing Out the Irons

When you hit an iron shot in golf, you are striving for one thing above all else: *accuracy*.

The woods give you distance. But the iron clubs enable you to pinpoint those approach shots to the green.

Strength and power off the tee won't do a bit of good unless you can follow up with crisp, accurate iron shots that put your ball close to the hole.

Accuracy, and not distance, should be your motto with the irons. It is the only way to good golf scores.

Generally speaking, the irons in your golf bag can be broken down into three main groups: long irons (No. 2-3-4), mid-irons (No. 5-6-7) and short irons (No. 8-9 and wedge).

Each of these clubs has a specific purpose. As a beginner, however, you probably will be concerned with only three or four of them. But we will describe all of them briefly anyway.

The No. 2 is the longest of the irons. It has a long shaft and an almost straight clubface. It gives you greater distance than any of the other irons. When you need a long ball off the fairway and the lie is too close for a wood, the No. 2 is your best bet.

The No. 3 and No. 4 irons are slightly shorter than the No. 2 and have more loft to the clubface. This means they don't carry as far, but they do get the ball much higher in the air.

It is difficult to say just how far these irons should propel your ball. Some folks are bigger and stronger than others.

Naturally, they hit the ball farther. But just to give you a general idea of the distances of the long irons, here is a flexible estimate:

No. 2—160 to 180 yards
No. 3—150 to 170 yards
No. 4—130 to 150 yards

In all likelihood, your first set of golf clubs won't include either the No. 2 or No. 4 irons. But this is all right. The No. 3 can get the job done just as well, It gives you almost the distance of the No. 2 iron and almost as much loft as the No. 4.

Non-experts would be wiser to stick for the most part to the middle distance irons—the No. 5-6-7. These clubs have shorter shafts, which make them easier to control. They are versatile clubs. They give you distance and loft.

More importantly, the mid-irons give the average golfer more confidence than the longer clubs. With a No. 2 iron, you are apt to be worried about the success of your shot. With a No. 5, however, most players feel they can hit a good shot more often than not.

Although the No. 5, 6 and 7 irons can send the ball as far as 150 yards, they also are valuable clubs at short range. Many pros use them for short little approach shots from the edge of the green.

The short irons, the No. 8, 9 and wedge, are sometimes called the "payoff" clubs. From 100 yards out to within a few feet of the cup, they are the instruments that put you close enough for those pars and birdies.

The No. 8 and 9 irons and the wedges are sharply-angled clubs. They are not designed for distance, but rather for loft and accuracy. They get you out of the trouble your other clubs get you into—sand traps, the rough, behind trees, etc.

No matter what iron you happen to be using, there are two important points to keep in mind: *firm grip* and *hit down on the ball*.

You will discover that irons sometimes turn in your hands

Lofted irons are designed to get you out of trouble.

at the moment of impact unless you have double checked your grip for firmness. Many poor iron shots are the result of the clubface being open or closed instead of square as it strikes the ball. This situation can be traced directly to a grip that is too loose. A crisp, accurate iron shot depends on the firmness and unity of your hands.

So, *check that grip!*

The second "must" concerning iron play is that *all* iron shots must be struck on the downswing. Here are several tips on how to hit down with your irons without making a conscious effort to do so:

Firm grip is necessary for all iron sho

Always keep the clubface "square" to the ball on iron shots.

Keep the weight evenly distributed or perhaps a little more on the left foot.

Keep your hands slightly ahead of the ball at address.

Never try and lift the ball with your hands.

Let the clubhead do the lifting.

Because your No. 2, 3 and 4 irons have long shafts, it may help you to play the ball more toward your front (or left) foot when using these clubs. When swinging the No. 5, 6 or 7 irons, move the ball back toward the center of your stance.

Here is the general rule to help you remember where to position the ball for iron shots:

The higher the iron, the farther back you play the ball.

Follow this advice and you will find that you are hitting down on the ball just the way the pros do.

Stance, of course, varies with the club. Long iron shots call for a square stance. A semi-open stance, with the left foot drawn back, is advisable for the middle-distance irons. As you move into the short iron range, your stance narrows—that is, you keep your feet closer together than in a regular stance. The short iron stance also is open.

It is very likely that you will develop your own stance as you progress in golf. Many of the top pros differ in their theories on stance. But for the time being, make an effort to follow these suggestions until you have learned to hit the ball. There will be plenty of time for experimenting later on.

The short approach shot is golf's great equalizer. A good approach makes up for bad drives and errant second shots. No shot can save you as many strokes as the approach.

By definition, an approach shot is any shot hit toward the green from 40 or 50 yards out on the fairway—or right from the edge of the green, maybe 10 or 15 feet from the cup. It is a stroke which calls for finesse, control, timing and "feel."

There are two types of approach shots—the pitch and the pitch-and-run—but many beginners often confuse them.

The pitch is a high, lofty shot to the green using the No. 8, No. 9 or pitching wedge, depending on distance. It is usually hit with a full, firm swing. In most cases, the height will enable you to make the ball stop on the green. But still you must attempt to hit down on the ball to give it maximum backspin. When the ball lands on the green, this spinning effect causes it to "grab" and stop after several bounces instead of rolling past the cup. The pitch shot is particularly valuable when there are obstructions such as trees, rocks and sand traps between you and the green. In such cases, the loft of the pitch shot will enable you to go over the trouble and land on the green. A last reminder about the pitch shot: hit down on the ball and trust the angle of the clubface to get it into the air. Don't try and lift it with your hands.

Pitch shots call for very little body movement. Remember: hit down on the ball.

The pitch-and-run is just the opposite of the pitch shot. Instead of trying for height, you hit the ball on a lower line and let it run (or roll) up to the pin. This shot can be used only when you have a clear, flat path to the green since the ball will not carry all the way in the air, it hits in front of the target and rolls the rest of the way. Thus, if there is a trap or a tree between you and the green, the pitch-and-run is not the shot to try. Go to your regular pitch shot and lift the ball over the obstructions.

Success or failure of the pitch-and-run shot depends a great deal on your choice of clubs.

The point to remember is that you don't need a lofted club like a No. 9 iron or wedge to hit a pitch-and-run shot. You are not going for height, so select a club with a less lofted club-face—maybe a No. 5 or No. 6 iron. Even a No. 7 will do the job nicely on a pitch-and-run approach.

The exact club you choose should be determined by the distance your ball lies from the cup. You want a club that gives you enough carry to reach the edge of the green so that the ball can roll toward the hole. A No. 6 will give you less loft but more roll than a No. 7. After practicing this shot for a while you will have a good idea of just what each club can do. And speaking of practice, there is no more important shot in golf than the pitch-and-run, so put as much time in on it as you can.

Using mid-irons like the No. 5 and No. 6 also is helpful in the event that you fail to hit the ball correctly. You can miss the shot with one of these clubs and still get enough roll on the ball to put you near the green. With a lofted club such as a No. 9, a missed shot simply pops up into the air and doesn't go very far.

The pitch-and-run shot is hit differently than the regular pitch shot. Here are some of the main points about the pitch-and-run approach:

Keep the feet closer together than in regular iron stance.

Use open stance with the left foot drawn back from line of flight.

On pitch-and-run shot, keep feet close together and use open stance. Choke up for better control.

Keep body perfectly still during the swing. Use arms only.

Wrists are held stiff during the swing, making the shot appear more rigid than usual.

Clubhead is taken back low and finishes low.

Follow-through should be same length as the backswing. Never take a full backswing and then "ease" into the ball. A firm finish promotes a firm shot.

Don't hit down on the ball as with the other iron shots. Instead, try to hit the ball cleanly off the turf. This gives over-spin instead of backspin and allows the ball to roll farther after landing on the green.

Choke up on the shaft of the club as much as you need to in order to feel comfortable and in control. The closer you are to the green, the more you should choke up.

In summing up these two types of approach shots, it might be well to note that while the high, floating pitch shot looks prettier, the simple pitch-and-run usually gets the job done just as efficiently—and with less chance of hitting a poor shot. Use whichever you think will get you closest to the pin. Always remember, however, to *take the easiest and safest route to the hole*.

But even the safest route may sometimes lead you into trouble—into a sand trap.

71

Since very few of us are fortunate enough to play a round of golf without hitting at least a few sand traps, it is important that you learn how to cope with this situation. Knowing how to blast out of the sand is a "must."

For some mysterious reason, sand trap shots seem to get most golfers upset psychologically. Many players "die" when they discover their ball lodged in the sand. They are beaten before they even swing the club in an effort to escape from the trap.

Beginners, then, should make an effort to look upon the sand trap shot as you would on any other shot. Don't talk yourself out of it!

The best club to use in the sand trap is the sand wedge, a specially designed club with a heavy head and a deeply-angled face which cuts through the sand and pops the ball into the air. If you don't have a sand wedge, however, a plain pitching wedge or even a No. 9 iron will do the trick.

In the final analysis, it is not the club that gets you out of the sand. It is your swing.

The stroke for the sand shot is best described as "lazy but firm." Play the ball off your front foot with an open stance. Take the clubhead back slowly and then hit down with good wrist action. But don't strike the ball. *Hit one or two inches behind the ball.*

This is what makes the sand trap stroke different than any other in golf. Instead of letting your clubhead strike the ball, you cut into the sand behind the ball. The sand then "explodes" under your ball and rides it up into the air.

The follow-through is the most important single phase of the explosion shot because it is the follow-through action of the hands and club that provides the cushion of sand on which the ball travels out of the trap. Hitting down into the sand and then quitting spells trouble.

The length of your backswing will determine how far the ball travels. If you are in a trap right next to the green, take a short, precise backswing and then hit through the sand with an exaggerated wrist movement. If you have 30 or 40 yards to travel out of a trap, take a longer backswing and hit closer to the ball—maybe one inch instead of two. This provides the carry you need to cover the distance to the green.

The only way to get the "feel" of the explosion shot is by practicing in a sand trap whenever you get the opportunity. Each time you blast out, you will acquire a little more of the skill, and confidence, necessary to execute this shot with success.

With experience you will learn that the lie and the texture of the sand tell you how far to hit behind the ball. For instance, if the sand is loose and dry, you must hit farther behind the ball than if the sand is wet and packed. Likewise, if the ball is partially buried, or plugged, you must hit closer behind the ball.

It is against the rules to ground your club in a trap. The club may not touch the sand until you swing at the ball. Thus, you must determine the texture of the sand as you walk into the trap. Set your feet well in the sand. Wiggle them into place as you address the ball. In most cases, your feet will tell you how soft or how hard the sand is. Then you can judge how far to hit behind the ball.

Of all the tips on how to hit out of a sand trap, however, the one mentioned earlier in this chapter is still the best:

Make yourself believe you can do it!

Chapter VIII

Putting Your Way to Par Golf

There is an old saying in golf that goes:

"You drive for show . . . but you putt for dough."

Which is another way of saying that putting is the payoff—that it is one of the most important and exacting phases of your game. Long, booming drives are impressive. Crisp, accurate iron shots are things of beauty. But the putt gets your ball into the hole. And that is the object of the game.

Par on most golf courses is 72. Exactly one half of that number of strokes needed for a perfect round is based on putts. In other words, 36 of the 72 strokes required for a round of par golf are taken on the putting green.

There are, naturally, endless variations of putting grips and stances. But it is a poor idea for you to copy someone else's style down to the last detail. It might not fit your needs.

The best idea is to experiment until you find the putting style best suited to you. Strive, above all, for relaxation and comfort. When you reach this point, you surely have found the best way for *you* to putt.

At the same time, though, there are some accepted fundamentals that will help you become a more accurate putter in a shorter space of time.

Study the following suggestions well, and then work them into your own technique when you practice putting.

STANCE:

Most top golfers advocate a narrow stance with the feet very close together. The exception to this is when you have a long putt. Then the stance may be widened for better balance and control. The weight should be evenly distributed, although many fine putters prefer to keep most of the weight forward—or on the left foot.

The ball is played off the left foot and no more than four inches from the left toe. Playing the ball close to the body in

this manner instead of reaching for it helps you keep your head and body directly over the ball as you putt. In this position, the arms are held close to the body and thus there is less chance of the wrists and arms moving off line during the putt.

Once you have decided where to play the ball in your individual style of putting, make sure you play it from the same spot everytime—whether you have a one-foot putt or a 30-footer. This way, you will retain a good idea of how hard the ball should be struck for putts of varying length.

The body and head must be kept perfectly still as you putt the ball, and even after the ball is on its way. Only the wrists and arms move as you putt. The slightest swaying of the body or the smallest movement of the head will throw your stroke off line. You will lose the "feel" of the putt—and, most usually, you will miss the hole.

So, keep that head and body still!

There is absolutely no reason for movement when you have to tap a golf ball only two or three feet. But surprisingly enough, many beginners are just as active when they putt as they are when they hit a 250-yard drive off the tee. A putt doesn't require strength or clubhead speed. It calls only for finesse and finger-tip control.

GRIP:

The grip which gives you the best "feel"—the best control and the most comfort—is the grip to use when putting. Like the stance, there are numerous variations of the grip. But again there probably is only one that will be best for you. Experiment until you find it.

In the meantime, remember that in the putt—as in all other golf shots—you must strive for *co-ordination and unity of the hands*.

A lack of co-operation between your hands can lead to all sorts of difficulties on the putting green.

According to golf's greatest putters—men like Walter Hagen, Bobby Jones, Horton Smith, Sam Snead and Billy Casper—each hand has a different role in the putt. The left hand acts as a guide. The right hand supplies the power. The hands, while performing different jobs, do not work independently of one another. They function as a unit. Each does its part in the putting stroke, but neither dominates the stroke.

As long as you are going to experiment with the various putting grips, you may as well begin with the one used by most of the pros—the reverse overlapping grip.

This grip, luckily, is a lot simpler than it sounds.

In the reverse overlapping grip, the index finger of the left hand overlaps the little finger of the right hand on the shaft. To take the reverse overlapping grip, follow these two simple steps:

1. Place both hands on the shaft of the putter as in the baseball grip.

2. Now lift your left index finger off the shaft and place it on top of the pinky of the right hand.

That's all there is to it.

Reverse overlapping putting grip.

Billy Casper, one of the finest putters among the pros, uses the reverse overlapping grip because, ". . . It tends to fuse the hands together, thus creating the feeling that two hands become one."

Of course, you may not prefer the reverse overlapping grip once you have tried it. If not, experiment with the regular overlapping grip, the interlocking grip or the plain baseball grip—all of which were described in Chapter Three.

Regular overlapping putting grip.

No matter which you choose, however, make sure you maintain a firm but relaxed hold on the shaft. A tense grip will spoil the rhythm of your putting stroke. A loose, sloppy grip is just as bad.

STROKE:

A putt can be stroked with either the wrists alone . . . or with wrist *and* arm action. Both styles are popular.

The wrist method confines the movement of the arms and lets the wrists move the clubhead. In the other style, the arms supply the movement while the wrists have less to do with the stroke.

Again, this is a case where you must experiment with the different types of putting strokes until you find the best one— the one that gets your ball in the hole most consistently.

All good putters agree that the blade must be *square to the line of the putt*. The face of the putter must be square at address, square on the backswing, square at impact and square as you finish the stroke. The slightest turning of the putter blade will push the ball off line.

Of equal importance, always *take the putter back low to the ground*. Never lift the putter blade with your hands. Take it away from the ball slowly, making certain to keep it close to the ground. If you take the putter back in this low groove, you find it easier to stroke the ball properly as you putt.

Another sound idea is to make your putting follow-through

about the same length as the backswing. For example, if your putter blade goes back eight inches, it should travel at least eight inches along the line of the putt *after* the ball has been struck. It is almost like the pendulum action we mentioned in Chapter Five.

In putting, distance is an important factor to consider when stroking the ball. Everytime you stand over a ball, you must ask yourself: How hard, or how easy, do I have to hit the ball to reach the cup?

A good motto to remember is: "Never up, never in." This means that if you don't get at least as far as the cup with your ball, you can never hope to sink the putt.

Always try to get close enough for an easy second putt even if you are off line. The line of your putts can be corrected. But distance is another thing. It is better to have your putt roll a few inches past the cup than have it stop several inches short. The short putts never drop. The long ones sometimes do.

On very long putts, it sometimes helps to picture an imaginary two-foot circle around the hole. Aim your first putt for the center of this circle. Even if you miss the cup, you are still in position to make your next putt if you have rolled the ball inside the circle.

What is the best way to line up a putt?

The most common method is to stand behind the ball and survey the distance to the hole, the roll of the green and other factors which may influence the ball once it is struck.

If you have a straight putt on a flat green, lining up the shot is a relatively simple matter. If, however, you have a sidehill or downhill lie on a sloping green—well, then you must take several things into consideration. How far to the right (or left) must I stroke the ball to make it break toward the cup? Is the green fast or slow? Is the grain with me or against me?

You must arrive at the answers to these questions before stroking the ball. It is part of the mental planning we discussed earlier.

As you become increasingly aware of factors affecting your putting, you will discover other things to consider. "Reading" the green is one of these.

If the green has been cut toward you and the blades of grass are leaning in the direction of your ball, the putt must be stroked more firmly to overcome resistance offered by the grass. If the blades of grass are leaning toward the hole, the ball naturally will roll faster so the stroke must be gentler. Similar compensations must be made if the grass is wet or dry; long or short, or if the ball lies on a slope.

With experience you will learn to cope with these various situations.

In the meantime, practice and patience will help you master the art of putting. It also will help if you review some of the points covered in this chapter.

1. Use a narrow stance for all but long putts.
2. Play the ball three or four inches off the left foot.
3. Never reach or stretch for the ball with a putter.
4. Choose the most comfortable and relaxed grip.

5. Remember hands must work as a unit.
6. Keep body and head perfectly still.
7. Keep putter blade square to the line of putt at all times.
8. Strive for low backswing and follow-through.
9. Be long rather than short on first putt.
10. "Read" the green carefully before putting.

In conclusion, seek the right mental outlook on putting. True, it is important. But it is not vital. Try to putt well. But consider putting as just another part of the game. Don't build up mental pressures. Treat putts as just another shot, no more, no less.

Chapter IX

Choosing Your Equipment

Buying a set of golf clubs can be as personal as buying a new suit. They've got to fit.

The best suggestion, of course, is to ask a golf professional to help you in your selection of new clubs.

Clubs are your tools of the trade. Like the carpenter who insists that his hammer have just the right weight and balance, you too must outfit yourself with clubs that feel like a part of you when you swing them.

If you happen to be one of those fortunate beginners who is able to buy a new set of golf clubs, there are certain general hints which can be of value.

The two most important things to consider in club-buying are:

1. *Length*
2. *Weight*

Clubs of the wrong length or incorrect weight can be detrimental to your progress in golf. You can't just pick up any club and hope to get the best results. Unfortunately, many beginners don't realize this. They start with a set of clubs that were built for someone else. The result is poor golf and aggravation instead of fun.

Proper length is determined mainly by two factors—the length of your arms and how far you stand from the ball at address.

A short player, contrary to common belief, usually takes long-shafted clubs. Why? Because his arms are shorter and in most cases he stands farther away from the ball than a taller player and he also takes a flatter swing. He must reach for the ball, so he needs longer clubs.

By contrast, most tall golfers stand closer to (or above) the ball and use an upright stance. Since tall players aren't required to reach or stretch for the ball, they can afford to swing shorter clubs.

The length of your clubs also can be based on how close your fingers are to the ground when you stand with your arms hanging naturally at your sides. Oddly enough, a six-footer's fingertips often are the same distance above the ground as are a five-footer's. In such cases, both could use clubs of identical length.

You can see from these illustrations that size can easily fool you in relation to buying golf equipment. Don't guess. Play it smart. Ask a pro to help you select the *right clubs*.

Length is measured in inches from the base of the clubhead to the tip of the shaft. The driver is the key to the length of the woods. The No. 2 iron indicates the length of your irons.

Generally speaking, men's drivers range in length from 42 inches to 43 inches. The No. 2 iron runs about 38 to 39 inches. Women's clubs, naturally, are slightly shorter. Their average length is 41 to 42 inches for the woods and 37 to 38 inches for the irons.

Unfortunately, many youngsters start playing golf with their father's clubs. These are usually too long and too heavy for them. Under such circumstances it is almost impossible for a youngster to get the proper feel with an adult's equipment. The best thing to do would be to ask Dad to buy himself a new set and let you have his clubs cut down to your size. Any pro will be glad to do the job.

After length, weight is the next factor to consider when buying golf clubs.

Overall weight is not important. It is the distribution of weight that makes the difference. This distribution is what gives the club balance and affects your "feel" or control.

Weight controls the tempo of your swing which, as you have learned, should be smooth and even from start to finish. If your clubs are too light for your size and strength, you will not be able to feel the clubhead as you swing. If the clubs are too heavy, you can't swing as quickly as desired, and you lose valuable clubhead speed.

If you must make a choice, however, between heavy and light clubs, choose the lighter clubs. You will get more whip and more wrist action. Playing will be easier than with a big, unwieldy club that makes you swing with arm power instead of rhythm and timing.

The distribution of weight between the clubhead and the shaft is known in golf as *swingweight*.

Or maybe the following explanation will make it clearer for you:

Swingweight is best described as the weight which a golfer feels in the head of the club when he swings it—as compared to the weight he feels when he simply picks up the club and holds it in his hands. There is a big difference.

When you buy a set of clubs, you will note that swingweight is designated by letters (A, B, C, D and E) and also by numbers (zero through 9). The important thing for the beginner to concern himself with, however, is the letter designation.

Here is a general breakdown of the various swingweights. See which group you fit into.

A and B swingweight—Very light, and used mainly by women, girls and small boys.

C swingweight — Medium swingweight favored by most women and many teenagers.

D and E swingweight—Heaviest. Designed for men but sometimes used by strong women professionals.

In the pro shop or golf store, you will see the swingweights labeled C-1 or C-5 or D-1. Don't worry about the numbers. Just make sure you select A, B or C swingweights to begin with. Then you can't go too far wrong.

Almost as vital as length and weight in buying golf clubs is *flexibility*.

Flexibility indicates the amount of bend or "whip" in the shaft of the club. This flexibility helps you get the "feel" of the clubhead as you swing. Flexibility might be compared to the bend in a light fishing rod, which whips back and forth as the angler makes his cast.

Some clubs have more flexibility than others—just as a deep sea fishing pole is stiffer and less flexible than a fly rod.

There are five basic flexibilities in golf clubs, designated as follows:

L or No. 4—Whippiest and most flexible of all shafts. Ideal for women, children and older golfers who must rely on "feel" rather than strength.

A or No. 3—Medium flexibility. Preferred by average women players and some teenagers.

R or No. 2—Medium stiff shaft used by a majority of weekend players, and a few of the stronger women players.

S or No. 1—A firm, strong shaft that should be used only by big, strong men.

X Shaft—Very stiff shaft with little noticeable flexibility. Not recommended for anyone other than an experienced player who knows what he is doing.

Obviously, youngsters should shy away from clubs other than those with L or A shafts. These give you all the whip you need in the beginning. You will have a better touch to your swing. Wait until you are older and stronger before promoting yourself to the R or S shafts.

Again, the best way to get proper flexibility is to let a pro watch you swing, and then take his advice. Fitting you with the right clubs is his business. He knows best.

Most iron clubs are of standard size and weight. With the wooden clubs, however, you have the option of buying a deep-faced club or a shallow-faced club. A deep face on your driver gives you more hitting surface than a narrower face. It is a good club for beginners. You can "miss" your drive and still get enough wood on the ball to send it 100 yards or so down the fairway.

A beginner need not worry about a full set of clubs. Two woods, the No. 1 and No. 3, are all you need for your tee shots and long fairway shots. As for the irons, you can get by with a No. 3, 5, 7 and 9 and, of course, the putter.

You can add other clubs as you go along. But keep things simple at the start. Don't bog yourself down with a lot of equipment that you don't need or, more importantly, that you

A light, easy-to-carry bag makes golf much more enjoyable.

are not sure how to use.

Another factor to consider is that you probably will be carrying your own bag most of the time. If it is too heavy, you will tire faster and golf will cease to be fun. A light bag and a minimum number of clubs will keep you fresh for the entire round.

In short, take every advantage you can. Golf is tough enough without making it any tougher by choosing the wrong equipment.

Twelve Points Dealing with Golf Etiquette

1. Be at the first tee, ready to play, at the agreed time.
2. Give all players, regardless of ability or sex, every courtesy.
3. If you are moving slowly or looking for a lost ball, allow the players behind you to go through.
4. Smooth out all footprints and club marks you have made before leaving a sand trap.
5. Park your golf cart to the side of a green while you are putting. Never pull a cart through a trap or across a green.
6. Replace all divots.
7. Delay play until the players in front of you are safely out of range.
8. Be on the alert to shout "Fore" should your ball appear to be headed for another player.
9. Do not scuff the green with your golf spikes.
10. Do not speak or otherwise annoy a player who is about to hit a shot.
11. Avoid standing in front of or directly behind a player while he is putting.
12. Leave the green promptly after holing out. You can mark your scorecard later.

GLOSSARY

Ace: Another term used to describe a hole-in-one.

Approach: A shot to the green, or putting surface, usually hit with a short or medium iron.

Away: Refers to the ball lying farthest from the hole when more than one golfer is playing.

Birdie: One stroke less than par on a hole.

Bite: The action imparted to a ball by backspin.

Bogey: One stroke over par on a hole.

Brassie: The No. 2 wood.

Bunker: Usually refers to a sand trap, but was originally a natural hazard on a golf course such as a large hill or mound.

Caddy: Person who carries a player's golf bag and clubs.

Caddy cart: A two-wheel cart used to haul golf clubs around the course.

Casual water: Temporary accumulation of water which is not regarded as a hazard.

Cleek: Originally the least lofted iron club except for the putter. Later developed as a wooden club with loft comparable to a No. 1 or No. 2 iron.

Club: The tool used to strike a golf ball. Also refers to an organization which provides golfing facilities for its members—that is, a golf club.

Course: The whole area on which golf play is permitted.

Divot: A small strip of turf torn loose by the club as it strikes down into the ball. This is known as "taking a divot."

Dormie: When one player is ahead of his opponent by as many holes as there are remaining to be played.

Driver: The No. 1 wood. Usually used only off the tee.

Eagle: Two strokes under par on a hole. A double eagle would be three strokes under par. Example: a golfer scores an eagle when he gets a three on a par-five hole.

Face: Striking surface of the clubhead. Also known as the clubface.

Fairway: The well-mowed portions of grass which lie between the teeing off area and the putting green.

Fore: A warning to a player ahead that a ball has been hit, or is about to be hit, in his direction. Comes from the original cry of "foreward."

Flagstick: A thin stick with a numbered flag which is placed in the cup to indicate the exact location of the hole on a green.

Foursome: A match in which two golfers compete against two others, or in which all four compete against each other.

Green: The well-manicured grass area used for putting.

Ground under repair: Any part of a golf course which is under construction or which in any way interferes with the natural process of play. Example: A pile of drainage pipes along the side of a fairway. Or maybe a ditch dug across a fairway to accommodate a new watering system. A ball may be removed from behind or in such ground under repair areas.

Halve: When opponents take the same number of strokes on a hole. Also known as a tie.

Hanging lie: When a ball rests on a downhill slope.

Hazard: Any bunker, water (except casual water), bare patches, scrapes, roads, tracks and paths.

Head: Part of the club which strikes the ball, as distinguished from the shaft.

Heel of the club: Part of the club where the shaft joins the clubhead.

Hole: The cup into which you try and putt the ball on the green. Usually 4¼ inches in diameter and at least four inches deep.

Hole high: When an approach shot is hit as far as the hole but off to one side.

Hole out: The act of putting the ball into the cup to finish play on a hole.

Honor: The privilege of playing first off the tee, usually accorded to the player who has won the preceding hole.

Hook: A ball which travels in a curving line to the left of the target.

Iron: A club with a metal head. (No. 1, 2, 3, 4, 5, 6, 7, 8, 9, pitching wedge, sand wedge and putter.)

Lie: Manner in which the ball rests on the ground after being hit.

Links: Term applied to a golf course which has been laid out without changing the natural contour of the landscape.

Loft: Angle of the clubface which helps get the ball into the air.

Marker: Signs, wooden stakes or round objects which are used to outline the limits of the driving area.

Mashie: An obsolete term for the No. 5 iron.

Match: Contest or competition between two or more players or sides.

Match play: Competition in which the results are determined by the number of holes won.

Medal play: Stroke competition in which results are determined by the total number of strokes taken for the whole round.

Nassau: A method of scoring: one point for the first nine, one point for the second nine, and one point for the entire 18 holes.

Neck: Part of the club where the shaft joins the head.

Obstruction: Anything artificial, whether constructed, erected, placed or left on the course which might interfere with play.

Open: A tournament open to both professionals and amateurs.

Out of bounds: Ground on which play is prohibited.

Par: A standard score for a hole as determined by the greens committee or builder of the course.

Penalty stroke: One stroke added to the score of a player or a team for violation of rules, etc.

Provisional ball: A ball played after a previous ball has been lost or hit out of bounds.

Push: A ball hit straight but off to the right of the intended line of flight.

Putter: Club used for putting on the green. Has no loft to clubface.

Rough: Deep grass lining the sides of the fairway or around the green.

Shaft: That portion of the golf club between the grip and the clubhead.

Shank: To hit the ball with the heel of the clubhead where it joins the shaft.

Slice: A shot which curves to the right of the target with a rapid spinning motion.

Sole: Bottom of the clubhead; that part which rests on the ground at address.

Spoon: The No. 3 wood. Used primarily for distance shots when the ball is resting on the fairway.

Square: A golf match that is all even—that is, tied.

Stroke play: Same as medal play, where the winner is the one who covers the 18 holes in the fewest number of strokes.

Stymie: Where one player's ball rests between the cup and the ball of another player.

Tee: Wooden peg upon which the ball is placed prior to teeing off with a driver.

Threesome: A match involving only three players.

Topping: Hitting only the top of the ball on the downswing thus causing a shot that rolls along the ground.

Twosome: A match involving one player against another.

Whiff: Missing the ball completely.

Wedge: A heavy soled, highly lofted iron club used for hitting out of deep rough or sand traps.

Index